The main theme of the house decorations, dating from 1854, is a reproduction of a big forest with acanthus leaves depicted in the papier-mache decorations, subsequently enriched with 23-carat gold leaf worked using the quartz technique and polished with agate.

The paintings outside the boxes have cherubs with musical instruments or in playful mood. The first tier also includes the profiles of classical poets, while the second features six allegories representing History, Poetry, Philosophy, Comedy, Tragedy and Music. On the third tier there are some *putti* holding tablets engraved with the titles and authors of 14 of the most important operas staged in this opera house.

A significant innovation in the appearance of the house was made by the radical change of colour inside the individual boxes. The original shade of beige has now been replaced by a blue-green pastel colour.

The current access to the stalls was designed by the engineer Miozzi in 1937 and decorated at the sides with two plaster caryatids.

The house originally had two small entrances in the section now occupied by the first box on the left and the first on the right of the current access, which until the second half of the 1930s was taken up by three boxes in the first tier.

The orchestra pit now has a moveable platform. When the pit is not required by the musicians, the platform can be raised to the level of the stalls floor, allowing some front rows of additional seats to be added, increasing capacity by 104. In this case the house capacity rises to 1126. The moveable platform, which consists of two elements, can also be completely or partially raised to the level of the stage in order to enlarge it.

The curtain was reproduced on the basis of an examination of the historic documentation, in dark-green, deep nap, fire-resistant, synthetic velvet decorated with 1100 flowers in gilt leather.

The new stage is accompanied by a second lateral stage onto which the stage equipment now moves sideways for construction and handling of the scenery.

previous pages:
The stage with curtain in velvet and gilt leather flowers

The Three Graces, ceiling decoration detail

One of the Nereids decorating the ceiling cornice in the house

External decorations on the second, third and fourth tiers of boxes

The place of honour in the house had a tormented existence, relating not only to the history of the opera house but also to the political and historic events of the city of Venice.

The royal box was not part of Giannantonio Selva's original plan for the Fenice; at the time of its construction the house contained only boxes of the same size.

Venice had lost its independence in May 1797 to Napoleonic France, which then handed the city over to the Austro-Hungarian empire for eight years following the Treaty of Campoformido in 1797, and in 1805 Venice once again came under French rule. The first imperial loggia was built only provisionally in 1807 to accommodate the emperor, Napoleon Bonaparte, who was expected in the opera house on Tuesday 1 December 1807 for a performance of the cantata *Il Giudizio di Giove* by Lauro Corniani Algarotti. Its construction required the demolition of three central boxes in both the second and third tiers.

In 1808 the architect Giannantonio Selva built the definitive model with the assistance of Giuseppe Borsato on the decorations. This was destroyed by the fire that struck the Fenice in December 1836, and was rebuilt along with the rest of the house by the Meduna brothers in 1837, with the assistance of Borsato, who increased the splendour of the decorations.

Following the Congress of Vienna in 1815, Venice once again found itself under Habsburg rule. At the end of March 1848, following insurrectionary uprisings and the Republic of Venice's consequent declaration of independence from Austria, the loggia was taken down so that the original tiers of boxes could be reinstated in the so-called 'Republican' house. The six boxes that had been in the centre of the house until the beginning of the nineteenth century were therefore rebuilt. However, the 'Imperial Austrian Royal Government' then returned, and on 22 August 1849 ordered reconstruction of the loggia in its original form. The decorations were entrusted once again to Giuseppe Borsato who, now over 70, remade them to a richer design than before. This was his last work; his box was presented in January 1850 in the presence of his widow Maria Bonadei Borsato.

The imperial loggia finally became the royal box in 1866 with the Veneto's entrance into the Kingdom of Italy.

The symbol of the Italian royal family can still be seen inside the box, reproduced on the side walls. There was a third Savoy shield on the crown of the external cornice, but this was removed after the republican victory in the referendum of 2 June 1946 and replaced with the lion of St Mark, the symbol of Venice.

There are some ivory-painted wooden *putti* in the corners of the walls on four gilt, wooden candelabra. On the papier-mache decorated wooden ceiling there is a reproduction of the painting *Apotheosis of the Sciences and the Arts*, originally by the painter Leonardo Gavagnin.

The royal box also offers its guests the use of a private room, which has its own private entrance.

The main access to the house with the royal box

The *Sale Apollinee*, so named because dedicated to the Greek god Apollo, father of the Muses and patron of the Arts, including music, consist of five rooms whose current layout dates from 1937.

These rooms are now used during the intervals by the audience occupying the first three tiers of boxes and the stalls.

They were originally used even when there were no shows in the opera house. The *Sale Apollinee* bar then also stayed open during the day and there was a billiard table in one of the rooms.

Unlike the house, which was completely destroyed by the enormous fire of 1996, about a fifth of these rooms survived. The surviving fragments can be easily recognised, as the precise intention of the reconstruction work was that it highlight the difference between the historic sections and the recent additions. The original parts of the ceiling cornices and remaining ornamental stuccoes on the walls are darker in colour, in testimony of the last fire. The same difference can be seen in the marble frames of some of the doors, repaired with new marble of a different colour, and in the new flooring, which merges with the typical 'Venetian terrazzo' that remained in the room dedicated to the famous singer Maria Malibran.

Thanks to these completions, the Sale Apollinee have been rebuilt on the basis of the originals, though a wider range of choice was conceded than in the house, shown by the new upholstery and furnishings in these rooms.

The Sala Dante

The main bar is in the Sala Dante, named after the frescoes that once decorated its walls.

This room was inaugurated in 1865 on the occasion of the sixth centenary of the birth of Dante Alighieri and, to celebrate the event, the painter Giacomo Casa created a large composition within the big decorative ceiling frame, showing Italy in the act of crowning the great poet; and six tempera fresco paintings on the walls, with the same number of scenes from the *Divine Comedy*. Two of these were then replaced in 1867 with others in tempera by Antonio Ermolao Paoletti.

In September 1976 the walls and ceiling of this room, renamed the Sala Guidi, were decorated with works by the Venetian painter Virgilio Guidi, which covered the scenes from Dante.

The fire of 1996, however, destroyed these canvases, bringing back to light some fragments of the original decoration by Casa, which have now been completed with a sinopia to assist their reading.

The Sala Dante with frescoes by Giacomo Casa

The Sala Ammannati

The Sala Grande

The Sala Grande or ballroom is the main room of the five Sale Apollinee, lit by the three windows in the middle of the entrance facade.

Used over the years for different purposes, the Sala Grande was an elegant venue for balls, chamber music concerts and conferences, but also for musicians' rehearsals, before La Fenice was provided with special rooms for these. It was also used by the governing board of the association that owned the opera house, which held its meetings here before transferring ownership to the Comune di Venezia in 1935.

Almost completely destroyed on the night of 29 January 1996, the Sala Grande has been faithfully reconstructed to the original model. The floor, which is above the foyer, collapsed after the fire and only the corners were saved. The current floor has been faithfully rebuilt to the original model and its characteristic floral patterns reproduced, requiring the use of various types of wood: maple, olive and cherry. The colour of the walls is also the same as the original.

A gallery runs right around the circumference of the upper part of the room, with access from the three doors on the top floor, in the gods bar.

The Sala Ammannati

The Sala Grande

'As it was, where it was', the motto for reconstruction of La Fenice, called for the opera house to be rebuilt as it was before the 1996 fire. This principle, however, was seen as applying only to the rooms of particular historic and artistic importance.

The opportunity was therefore taken to redesign the parts of the building that did not come into this category, resulting in the creation of three new rooms.

The Sala Rossi

The Sala Rossi is the most important new addition in this latest reconstruction. Situated in the south wing of the building, it is part of a section recently acquired by the opera house. It is dedicated to the memory of the architect Aldo Rossi, who died a year after drawing up the plans for the new La Fenice, which already included this space.

It is decoratively distinguished by a 2:3 scale reproduction of the facade of the Basilica Palladiana in Vicenza, built in cypress wood and covering the entire wall facing the entrance. This is intended as a tribute to one of the greatest architects of the Veneto, linking the new La Fenice to its cultural hinterland, but at the same time referring to the Teatro Olimpico in Vicenza, also by Palladio.

That Renaissance theatre is noted for its system of permanent wings in wood, carved and painted to resemble marble to give the effect of a town. In this case, the reproduction has been left in raw wood to indicate that it is a citation.

This new multi-function room is able to accommodate the choir

The Sala Rossi with the reproduction of the Basilica Palladiana facade in Vicenza

and the entire orchestra for rehearsals. But it will mainly host chamber and contemporary music concerts, given its fine acoustics and seating capacity of 190.

The acoustics were carefully studied in order to give the best possible sound response; indeed, this is very similar to that of the house itself.

The Sala Rossi may also be used as a recording studio.

Thanks to the reopening of the so-called 'water door' at the rear of the building, which had fallen into disuse over recent decades, this room has its own independent entrance. The public can therefore gain entrance without having to go through the main door, by crossing a bridge and a small *fondamenta* that have recently been named after Maria Callas.

The canal in front of this second entrance was excavated at the time Selva built the original Fenice, in line with what had been specifically called for in the competition. Indeed, as in the past, all transport in Venice is still water-borne and construction of the canal at the back of the new opera house was and remains indispensable to its operation.

The water entrance and bridge recently named after Maria Callas

The gods bar
and rehearsal room

next pages:
The house ceiling

The gods bar / Rehearsal room

This new room on the top floor of the Sale Apollinee was originally used both as the Gods Bar and as a storeroom. It is now a single space with a dual function: when the opera house is open to the public it acts as the Gods and Gallery Bar; when the opera house is closed it becomes a Musicians and Direction Rehearsal Room. Its patrons can also look out from a gallery running right around the perimeter of the Sala Grande Apollinea, accessed through three doors in front of the bar.
The room is distinguished by big wooden ceiling trusses and an oak planked floor.

The exhibition room / Rehearsal room

This other new room, originally used as a workshop for the production of stage scenery, is in the attic above the new gods bar. As the scenery is no longer made on the premises, it was decided to use this space as a dance rehearsal room. It is also intended as the venue for any exhibitions the opera house may decide to present.
The room is distinguished by some big windows offering a fine view over the roofs of Venice.

Chronology

16 MAY 1792
La Fenice opera house, designed by Giannantonio Selva, is opened after 18 months' work.

1 DECEMBER 1807
Demolition of the six central boxes and construction of the imperial loggia for Napoleon Bonaparte's visit to the opera house.

26 DECEMBER 1808
Unveiling of the new decorations in the house.

27 DECEMBER 1828
Unveiling of the remade decorations in the house.

13 DECEMBER 1836
A violent fire destroys the opera house.

FEBRUARY 1837
Reconstruction works begin to a plan by the Meduna brothers.

26 DECEMBER 1837
Opening of the new opera house.

JANUARY 1850
Reconstruction of the new imperial loggia, demolished the previous year following Venice's declaration of independence from Austria.

26 DECEMBER 1854
Unveiling of the last, definitive reworking of the the house decorations.

1865
To mark the sixth centenary of the birth of Dante Alighieri, six frescoes are painted in one of the first floor rooms depicting scenes from the *Divine Comedy*.

1866
The annexation of Venice to Italy is celebrated with a special evening attended by King Victor Emanuele II, the royal family and ministers of the new government.

1878
The fifth-tier boxes are converted into the gods.

1904
The fourth-tier boxes are converted into the Gallery.

23 JULY 1935
The box-holder owners of the opera house cede their shares to the Comune di Venezia.

1937
Upgrading and modernisation of the opera house to a plan by the engineer Miozzi.

1946
The lion of St Mark replaces the symbol of the Italian royal family in the cornice of the royal box.

SEPTEMBER 1976
New decoration of the Sala Dante by the painter Virgilio Guidi.

29 JANUARY 1996
The opera house is almost completely destroyed by arson.

14 DECEMBER 2003
Opening of the reconstructed La Fenice.

The opera house in figures

DIMENSIONS

Maximum length	c. 80 m.
Stalls	c. 255 m^2
Total volume	c. 160,000 m^3
Main stage	c. 511 m^2
Side stage	c. 200 m^2
Height of fly tower	c. 35.86 m
Proscenium	c. 11 x 13 m

CAPACITY

Stalls	326 seats
Orchestra pit	104 seats
1st tier of boxes	128 seats
2nd tier of boxes	146 seats
3rd tier of boxes	128 seats
Gallery	128 seats
Gods	166 seats
Total	1126 seats

CAPACITY OF THE OTHER ROOMS

Sala Rossi	190 people
Sala Grande and Sale Apollinee	330 people
Exhibition room	200 people

Bibliografia essenziale

1926
M.N. Mocenigo, *Il teatro La Fenice*, Venice.

1969
M.T. Muraro, *Le scenografie delle cinque prime assolute di Verdi alla Fenice di Venezia*, in *Verdi in Italia e nel mondo*, Primo Convegno internazionale di Studi verdiani, Parma.

1974
N. Mangini, *I teatri di Venezia*, Venice.

1987
M. Brusatin, G. Pavanello, *Il teatro La Fenice. I progetti, l'architettura, le decorazioni*, Venice.

1989
M. Girardi, F. Rossi, *Il teatro La Fenice. Cronologia degli spettacoli, 1792-1936*, Venice.

1992
L'immagine e la scena. Bozzetti e figurini dall'archivio del teatro La Fenice 1938-1992, ed. by M.I. Biggi, Venice.

M. Girardi, F. Rossi, *Il teatro La Fenice. Cronologia degli spettacoli, 1938-1991*, Venice.

1995
M.I. Biggi, *Giuseppe Borsato. Scenografo alla Fenice 1809-1823*, Venice.

1995-1996
F. Mancini, M.T. Muraro, E. Povoledo, *I teatri del Veneto, Venezia*, volume I, tome 1-2, Venice.

1996
M.I. Biggi, *Francesco Bagnara. Scenografo alla Fenice 1820-1839*, Venice.

1997
M.I. Biggi, *Il concorso per La Fenice 1789-1790*, Venice.

1998
M.I. Biggi, M.T. Muraro, *Giuseppe e Pietro Bertoja. Scenografi alla Fenice 1840-1902*, Venice.

2000
I progetti per la ricostruzione del teatro La Fenice 1997, Venice.

2001
Teatro Malibran. Venezia a San Giovanni Grisostomo, ed. by M.I. Biggi and G. Mangini, Venezia.

2003
A.L. Bellina, M. Girardi, *La Fenice 1792-1996. Theatre, music and history*, Venice.

La Fenice reconstructed 1996-2003. A building site in the city, ed. by L. Ciacci, Venezia.

ISBN 88-317-

€ 5,00

9 788831 788380